# REAL WORLD DATA

# GRAPHING HABITATS

Sarah Medina

Heinemann
LIBRARY

Chicago, Illinois

Customer Service  888–454–2279

Visit our website at www.heinemannraintree.com

Edited by Nancy Dickmann and Rachel Howells
Designed by Victoria Bevan and Geoff Ward
Original illustrations© Pearson Education Ltd
Illustrations by Geoff Ward
Picture research by Hannah Taylor

Originated by Modern Age
Printed and bound in China by Leo Paper Group

13 12 11 10 09
10 9 8 7 6 5 4 3 2 1

**Library of Congress Cataloging-in-Publication
Data**
Medina, Sarah, 1960-
  Graphing habitats / Sarah Medina.
    p. cm. -- (Real world data)
  Includes bibliographical references and index.
  ISBN 978-1-4329-1520-9 (hc) -- ISBN 978-1-
4329-1535-3 (pb)  1. Habitat (Ecology)--Juvenile
literature.  I. Title.
  QH541.14M43 2008
  577.072′8--dc22
                                    2008008458

**Acknowledgments**
The publishers would like to thank the following
for permission to reproduce photographs:
©Alamy p. 7 (Karel Lorier); ©ardea.com
pp. 8 (Stefan Myers), 20 (Chris Harvey);
©Corbis p. 25 (Paulo Fridman); ©FLPA
pp. 6 (Minden Pictures/Thomas Mangelsen),
9 (Minden Pictures/Mitsuhiko Imamori), 10
(Mike Lane), 12 (Minden Pictures/Michael
Durham), 13 (Chris & Tilde Stuart), 15
(Minden Pictures/Fred Bavendam), 16 (Minden
Pictures/Michio Hoshino), 18 (Mike Amphlett),
23 (Phil McLean), 24 (Minden Pictures/Jim
Brandenburg); ©Getty Images p. 26 (Taxi/
Stuart O'Sullivan); ©naturepl.com p. 22 (Pete
Oxford); ©Photolibrary p. 19 (Animals Animals/
Dominique Braud); ©Science Photo Library
pp. 4 (Cheryl Power), 14 (Nigel Cattlin).

Cover photograph of coral reef, reproduced with
permission of ©Getty Images (Digital Vision).

Every effort has been made to contact copyright
holders of any material reproduced in this book.
Any omissions will be rectified in subsequent
printings if notice is given to the publishers.

The publishers would like to thank Harold Pratt
for his assistance in the preparation of this book.

**Disclaimer**
All the Internet addresses (URLs) given in
this book were valid at time of going to press.
However, due to the dynamic nature of the
Internet, some addresses may have changed, or
sites may have changed or ceased to exist since
publication. While the author and publishers
regret any inconvenience this may cause readers,
no responsibility for any such changes can be
accepted by either the author or the publishers.
It is recommended that adults supervise children
on the Internet.

# CONTENTS

Some words are printed in bold, **like this**. You can find out what they mean by looking in the glossary, on page 30.

Earth is full of life! Plants and animals are all living things. Plants, such as flowers and trees, usually grow in soil or water. Animals, such as **mammals**, insects, reptiles, birds, and fish, live on land or in water.

A single living being is called an **organism**. A **species** is a group of plants or animals that are similar to each other in important ways. Members of a species can reproduce with each other, which means that they can have young. However, they may look very different in terms of some details. Happy-face spiders all have eight legs, a small head, and a large, round body. But some happy-face spiders have red, black, and yellow bodies, while others have yellow bodies with black spots.

No one knows exactly how many plant and animal species exist on Earth. So far, scientists have identified more than 1.5 million species, but there may be millions more.

 Different species depend on each other for survival. Many butterflies would die without the sweet nectar from flowers.

# What are graphs?

Graphs are a way to show information visually and without using a lot of words. There are many different types of graphs, but they all make it easier to see patterns at a glance. One type, a pie chart, shows the different parts of a whole picture. The table below shows the numbers of plant and animal species discovered in the world so far. The pie chart turns these numbers into percentages. The red section of the pie chart shows that 19 percent of all species are plants. The blue section shows that the rest are animals. You can easily see that there are many more groups of animals than plants on Earth.

| Species | Number in the world |
|---------|---------------------|
| Animals | 1, 249,000 |
| Plants | 287,655 |
| Total | 1,536,655 |

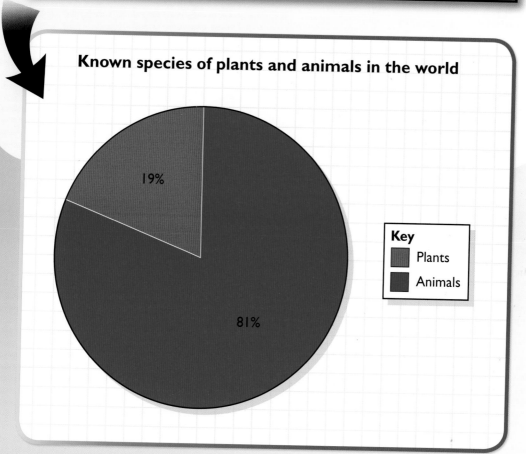

**Known species of plants and animals in the world**

19%

81%

**Key**
Plants
Animals

# A PLACE TO LIVE

Plants and animals live in all sorts of places—from the bottom of oceans to the tops of mountains. People can see plants and animals in gardens and parks, in towns and the countryside, and even in their own homes.

An **ecosystem** is an area where certain plants and animals all live together. Some ecosystems, such as **rain forests** and oceans, are huge. Others are smaller. A rain forest ecosystem contains thousands of different **organisms**, including different **species** of trees, flowers, **fungi**, insects, birds, and **mammals**. All the organisms that live in an ecosystem need each other to survive.

 In a wood ecosystem, plants such as trees and animals such as owls rely on each other for life.

 Even rotting vegetables are habitats for animals such as worms.

# Habitats

Ecosystems can contain several different habitats. A habitat is the particular place where a plant or animal lives. Like ecosystems, some habitats are large and others are small.

A good habitat must have everything an organism needs for life. Different organisms have different needs. All organisms need water and the right type of food. They may also need soil, shelter, space, and sunlight. Temperature and the amount of sunlight, rainfall, or wind are important factors, too. An ideal habitat provides the perfect conditions for a species' survival.

## Forest land

Forests cover more than 30 percent of Earth's land. More than half of all the world's species live in tropical rain forests.

Different plants and animals need different habitats. Polar bears need to live in a cold habitat, not a hot habitat. Water lilies need to live in water, not on land. If we take a plant or animal out of its natural habitat, it may die because it cannot find the food and shelter it needs.

Habitats for plants and animals are all around us. Some are large, and others are small. Some are on land, and others are in water. Whatever a habitat is like, it has the right conditions for the **organisms** that live there.

## Types of habitats

Mountains, deserts, **grasslands**, **wetlands**, forests, oceans, lakes, and **polar regions** are all large **ecosystems** with many different habitats. Antarctica, which is bigger than the United States, contains many habitats for many different organisms. Antarctica is the coldest, windiest, and driest continent on Earth. It is almost completely covered with thick snow and ice. No one would imagine that this harsh place could support life. But the Antarctic contains the ideal habitats for many organisms, including plants such as **lichens** and animals such as whales, fish, and penguins.

The icy Antarctic is a great habitat for penguins.

Small habitats are easy to spot. Lawns and flower beds in a school playground, park, or backyard are all habitats. A stone is a habitat for plants, such as moss, and insects, such as woodlice. Rock pools and sand dunes are seaside habitats. Fields and trees in the countryside are habitats, too.

## Carroll diagrams

A Carroll diagram can be used to display and categorize information clearly and simply. It looks a bit like a table. This Carroll diagram categorizes ecosystems and habitats according to whether they are on land or in water. Each ecosystem and habitat is put under the correct heading: land or water. We can now quickly see which category each ecosystem or habitat belongs to.

 Grasshoppers thrive in grasslands, where they can find all the food they need to survive.

### Ecosystems and habitats on land or in water

|  | Land | Water |
|---|---|---|
| **Ecosystems** | Forest<br>Desert<br>Grassland<br>Mountain | Ocean<br>Lake<br>River<br>Canal |
| **Habitats** | Tree<br>Lawn<br>Sand dune<br>Flower pot | Stream<br>Pond<br>Puddle<br>Bird bath |

# OBSERVING HABITATS

The best way to learn about habitats is to go out and look at them. This hands-on approach is a fun way to improve observation skills. It helps us to understand more easily what a habitat looks like, what lives there, and why those things live there.

Habitats to explore can be found in many places, such as a school playground or garden. A pond is an interesting habitat to observe. A pond is a pool of still, fresh water that forms when rainwater fills up a hole in the ground. Some ponds are quite large and survive for months or years. Others are tiny pools that only last for a few days. Plants and animals quickly appear in a new pond, because it provides the right type of food, protection, and shelter they need.

Many different **species** of plants and animals can be observed in a pond habitat, including grass, flowers, fish, frogs, snails, birds, and insects.

 Ponds are ideal habitats for all sorts of **organisms**, such as water lilies and frogs.

# Bar charts

A bar chart is a type of graph that helps to compare information about separate things. It can show at a glance how many animals are observed in a habitat. The table below shows the number of different animals observed in a pond habitat. The bar chart turns this information into a visual form. The horizontal line on the bar chart, called the **x-axis**, shows the names of the animals. The vertical line, called the **y-axis**, shows the numbers of animals seen. The tallest bar shows which animal was the most common in the pond habitat.

| Animal | Number seen |
|---|---|
| duck | 8 |
| frog | 3 |
| tadpole | 10 |
| pond snail | 2 |
| water beetle | 4 |
| dragonfly | 2 |

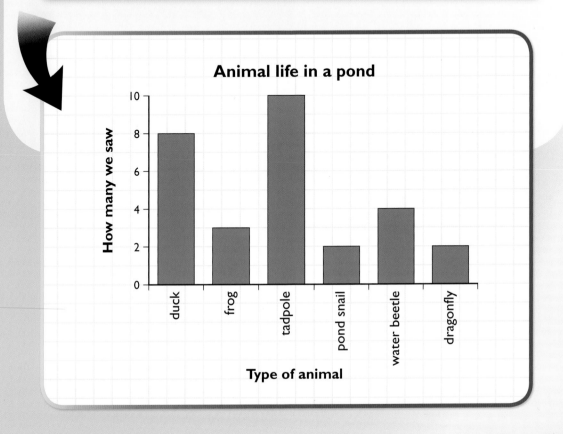

**Species** can only survive if they are suited to where they live. To do this, they adapt in different ways. This means that they change their structure so that they can survive in their habitat. **Adaptation** helps plants and animals to obtain the food they need, to build homes, and to stay safe. Adaptation also helps them to cope with different weather conditions and to attract **mates**. If a plant or animal species does not adapt, it may die out.

Species adapt over long periods of time by changing the way they look or behave. Owls have adapted to have soft, fluffy fringes on their wings, which help them to fly silently, so they can catch their **prey** without being heard.

Some animals, such as chameleons and hares, have adapted so their color can help them to blend in with their habitat. This makes them hard to see and keeps them safe from **predators**. It also helps them to catch their prey more easily.

 Bat adaptations have made it possible for them to hunt for insects in total darkness.

 Camels have adapted perfectly to survive in hot, dry, and sandy deserts.

## The case of the camel

Camels are one type of animal that has adapted to live in a harsh environment. This table shows some of the ways that camels have adapted to survive in harsh deserts. It organizes the information so that it is easy to see which feature of the habitat each adaptation relates to.

| Desert condition | Camel adaptation |
|---|---|
| sandy | • hairy ears to keep sand out<br>• long eyelashes to protect eyes<br>• nostrils that close to keep sand out of nose<br>• wide feet to walk more easily |
| hot and dry | • do not pant or perspire, which conserves water in body |
| prickly desert plants, such as cacti | • thick lips to protect mouth |
| little food | • one or more humps to store fat that can be used for energy |

People identify **species** by looking at the similarities and differences between different **organisms**. Some plants, such as a daffodil, have a single flower on one stem. Others, such as a bluebell, have many small flowers, all close together. By comparing the two plants, we can decide if they are the same species or different species.

## Types of turtles

Turtles are reptiles that have many similar characteristics. All turtles have a large shell. They have webbed feet, which help them to swim. They also have long claws to help them climb out of water. We might think that all turtles are one species. In fact, there are as many as 300 different turtle species.

 This Chinese Oak silkworm moth can be identified by its large, feathery antennae.

Comparing the differences between turtles can help people to know which species they are looking at. Some turtles, such as the loggerhead sea turtle, live in the sea. They eat sea plants, such as seaweed, and sea animals, such as crabs. They grow to be 120 centimeters (47 inches) long.

Wood turtles live in woods, fields, or riverbanks. They eat berries and animals such as earthworms. They are smaller than loggerhead sea turtles—they only grow to be 23 centimeters (9 inches) long.

 The loggerhead sea turtle is just one of hundreds of species of turtle.

## Comparing turtles

A Venn diagram is a visual tool. It helps to organize information in order to compare two things. It has two circles, in two different colors, that overlap in the middle. In a Venn diagram, the separate parts of the circles show the differences between two organisms. The overlapping part of the circles shows similarities. This Venn diagram shows at a glance the similarities (green section) and differences between loggerhead sea turtles (yellow section) and wood turtles (blue section).

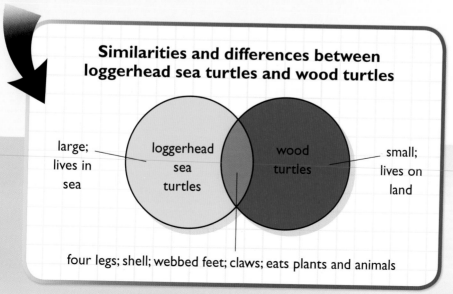

**Similarities and differences between loggerhead sea turtles and wood turtles**

large; lives in sea — loggerhead sea turtles

wood turtles — small; lives on land

four legs; shell; webbed feet; claws; eats plants and animals

All plants and animals need food for growth and life. An **organism** lives in a particular habitat because it can make or find the food it needs there. If a habitat has lots of food, the **population** of organisms living there will increase. If the food source is poor, an organism must move to a different habitat to find food.

A caterpillar eats green leaves. A caterpillar might live in a tree, which is its habitat. However, it will only live in a tree with lots of green leaves. If a tree does not have any green leaves, the caterpillar needs to move to another tree, or it may die.

## Helping animals

It can be hard for some animals to find enough food to eat, especially in winter. In harsh, cold weather, people can help animals, such as birds, by putting birdseed or nuts in the garden. This increases the birds' food source until the weather conditions improve.

 A caribou in Alaska eats fresh spring grass for growth and health.

# Line graphs

A line graph is used to show how something changes—for example, over a period of time. The line graph below shows how providing food for birds affects the number of birds seen in a garden. In week 1, no food is provided. In weeks 2 to 4, birdseed and nuts are provided. The table shows how many birds are seen in the garden in weeks 1 to 4. On the line graph, the **x-axis** shows the time. The **y-axis** shows the number of birds seen. Dots are placed on the graph and are then connected to make a line. The line goes up from left to right, showing that the number of birds increased over time.

| Week | Number of birds seen |
|------|----------------------|
| Week 1 | 12 |
| Week 2 | 18 |
| Week 3 | 25 |
| Week 4 | 35 |

# FOOD CHAINS

**Organisms** obtain energy from food in order to live. Plants make food from air, water, and sunlight. Animals eat plants or other animals, or both, to get the energy they need to live.

A **food chain** shows what eats what in a habitat. All food chains start with a plant, called a **producer**, that makes its own food. The next link in the food chain is a **consumer**. A consumer gets its energy from eating the producer or other consumers.

## Food chain links

Food chains can have different numbers of links. In many food chains, the producer is grass. The first consumer might be a grasshopper, which eats the grass. The next consumer could be a frog, which eats the grasshopper. The next consumer eats the frog, and so on, until the last consumer.

 In a garden habitat, a blackbird is a consumer that eats a worm.

Even if a consumer is not eaten by another animal, the chain still continues. **Decomposers** are tiny organisms that break down the dead bodies of consumers into simple **nutrients**. These nutrients go back into the earth, and plants use them to grow.

 Nutrients from dead organisms help living plants to grow.

## Types of eaters

Animals that eat plants are called **herbivores**. Cows are herbivores. So are elephants and many other types of animal. Animals that eat other animals are known as **carnivores**. Some large fish are carnivores—they often eat smaller fish. An animal that hunts and kills another animal is called a **predator**. The animal it eats is called **prey**. Animals that eat both plants and animals are called **omnivores**. For example, badgers eat fruit and worms.

### Direction of food chain, from the producer to the last consumer

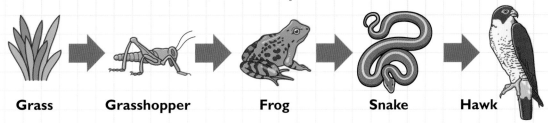

Grass     Grasshopper     Frog     Snake     Hawk

Producer                                               Last consumer

 A food chain is shown as a flowchart, which makes it easy to see what eats what. The arrows show the direction the food chain goes in, from the producer (grass) to the last consumer (hawk).

# FOOD WEBS

No matter what habitat they live in, all **organisms** are part of a **food chain**. A food chain is like a simple path that shows the relationships between the different organisms in a habitat. Each organism on the path finds food to obtain the energy it needs to survive, grow, and reproduce.

However, most organisms are part of more than one food chain. This is because a **producer**, such as grass, provides food for lots of different animals. Different animals, or **consumers**, may be eaten by several different animals, too. When food chains are linked, they are called a **food web**.

A food web is like a series of interconnected paths. Food webs show how different plants and animals are connected in lots of different ways. This helps them all to survive. Without each other, the different organisms may die.

## Top of the food chain?

Some animals are never killed for food by other animals. Lions, for example, are **predators**, but they are not **prey** to any other animal. They are at the top of the food chain. However, when lions die, **decomposers** still break down their bodies into **nutrients** for plants to grow.

 A lion is the last consumer in a food chain, because no other animal kills lions for food.

# Making the links

A diagram such as a food web organizes information. You could write a list of what eats what, but it is easier to understand this information when it is shown as a diagram. This food web contains seven different food chains, including the food chain from page 19. The food web shows that grass is eaten by beetles as well as grasshoppers. Grasshoppers are eaten by frogs—and by mice, too. Frogs are eaten by both snakes and lizards. And hawks, at the top of the food web, eat mice as well as snakes.

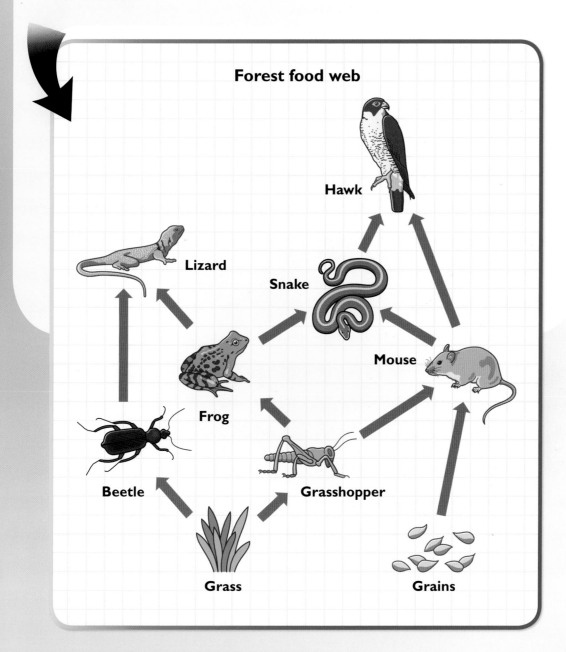

**Forest food web**

Hawk

Lizard

Snake

Frog

Mouse

Beetle

Grasshopper

Grass

Grains

# FINDING A BALANCE

**Organisms** that live in a habitat need each other to survive. If there is a change in the number of **species** in a habitat, the whole balance of life there can change. For example, when trees are cut down in a **rain forest** habitat, the organisms that rely on them for food and shelter may die.

Plants and animals that are introduced to a habitat, called "alien" species, may take over and drive out other, **native** species. In North Australia in 1935, a species of beetle was destroying sugarcane crops. Farmers introduced giant marine toads from South and Central America to

eat the beetles. They did eat the beetles. Unfortunately, they also ate other insects, fish, birds, and small **mammals**. Because the toads have no natural **predators**, they are still spreading and destroying native Australian species.

Another alien species is the American gray squirrel. These squirrels were introduced to England in 1876. Since then, England's native red squirrels have been almost completely wiped out. One reason is because gray squirrels live in the same habitats as red squirrels, and they compete with them for food.

 Alien giant marine toads have caused serious problems for several native species in Australia.

Red squirrel numbers have dropped in England since the alien gray squirrel was introduced.

# Double line graphs

A double line graph is similar to a line graph, but it has two lines instead of one. It is a useful way to show how more than one thing changes over time. It can show how one factor affects another. The table shows the numbers of squirrels counted in one forest in England over a period of time. When the information is made into a double line graph, it shows that as the number of alien gray squirrels increased, the number of native red squirrels went down.

| Month | Number of red squirrels | Number of gray squirrels |
|---|---|---|
| Spring 1996 | 50 | 20 |
| Fall 1996 | 40 | 35 |
| Spring 1997 | 30 | 45 |
| Fall 1997 | 20 | 60 |

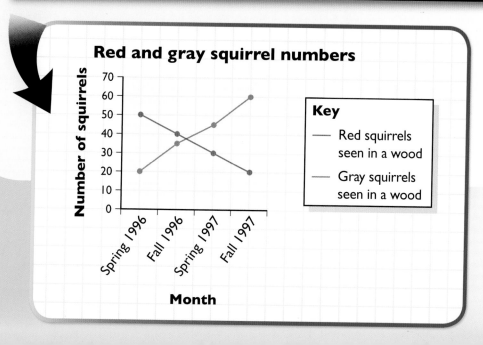

**Red and gray squirrel numbers**

Key
— Red squirrels seen in a wood
— Gray squirrels seen in a wood

# HABITATS UNDER THREAT

Habitats are very sensitive. Even small changes can affect them. If a pond has a tree above it, the tree shades the **organisms** that live in the pond. The tree habitat also provides food and shelter for insects, birds, and small **mammals**. If someone cuts the tree down, this habitat is lost.

Cutting down the tree also affects the pond habitat. Some organisms in the pond may need shade to survive. Cutting down the tree allows more sunlight to reach the pond water. This may kill some organisms or allow new, sunlight-loving organisms to move in.

## Habitat destruction

Too many changes to a habitat can completely destroy it. Much habitat destruction is caused by humans. Humans often destroy habitats, such as forests, for farming and **industry**, and to build homes. The **pollution** they create also causes habitat destruction.

Habitat destruction can wipe out plant and animal **species**. Already, many species have become **extinct**. The golden toad was a beautiful, bright orange toad that lived in Costa Rica. It became extinct in 1989, because of pollution.

Habitat destruction by humans is threatening species such as polar bears.

 Deforestation destroys many habitats, wiping out the organisms that live in them.

## The Amazon rain forest

The world's **rain forests** are home to millions of plants and animals. However, **deforestation** is destroying many rain forests, threatening thousands of species. In South America, deforestation is reducing the size of the Amazon rain forest, the world's largest rain forest. This area is measured below in hectares. (1 hectare equals 2.47 acres.) The table shows the number of hectares of rain forest over three years. The line graph uses the same figures to show at a glance how the Amazon rain forest is shrinking rapidly.

| Year | Hectares of Amazon rain forest remaining |
|------|------------------------------------------|
| 1990 | 520,027,000 |
| 2000 | 493,213,000 |
| 2005 | 477,698,000 |

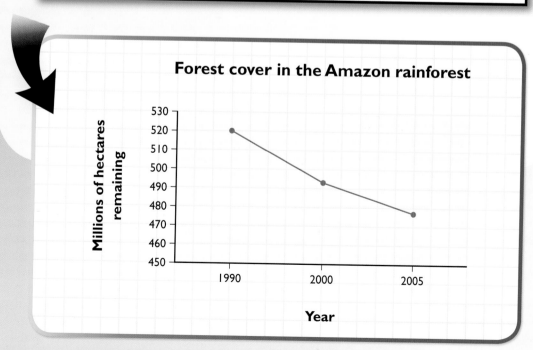

**Forest cover in the Amazon rainforest**

Earth is home to millions of **species**, including humans. Unfortunately, humans often destroy the world's habitats and cause species to become **extinct**. For example, orangutans are **mammals** that live in **rain forests** in Borneo and Sumatra, in Indonesia. **Deforestation** is destroying the orangutans' habitat.

**Conservation** means working to protect habitats and the plants and animals that live in them. Fortunately, many organizations across the world are involved in conservation work. Greenpeace, for example, is working on a project to end the deforestation of the Amazon rain forest by 2015.

## Our amazing Earth

It is impossible to count all the species that exist—or even the habitats they live in. We live on a rich and varied planet. But it is up to us look after our amazing Earth. Everyone can help to protect and look after habitats. People of all ages can join or give money to conservation projects. They can plant flowers to provide food for insects or clear away garbage, so that plants and animals can thrive.

 Planting new trees is a great way to protect habitats.

# Double bar charts

Like a bar chart, a double bar chart helps compare information. However, in a double bar chart, it is possible to include information for more than one place or time. This double bar chart shows the numbers of orangutans in Borneo and Sumatra in two different years. The **x-axis** shows the names of the islands and the **y-axis** shows the numbers of orangutans. The key shows that the blue bar is for 1930 and the red bar is for 1998. You can see that the numbers have fallen significantly. Many conservation workers are trying to save the orangutan from extinction.

| Location | 1930 | 1998 |
|---|---|---|
| Orangutan numbers in Borneo | 203,000 | 15,000 |
| Orangutan numbers in Sumatra | 69,000 | 12,000 |

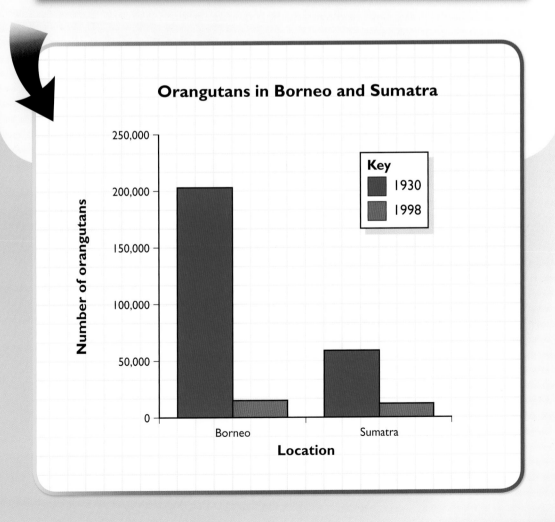

# Chart Smarts

**Data** is information about something. We often get important data as a mass of numbers, and it is difficult to make any sense of them. Graphs and charts are ways of displaying information visually. This helps us to see relationships and patterns in the data. Different types of graphs or charts are good for displaying different types of information.

## Pie charts

A pie chart is used to show the different parts of a whole picture. A pie chart is the best way to show how something is divided up. These charts show information as different sized portions of a circle. They can help you compare proportions. You can easily see which section is the largest "slice" of the pie.

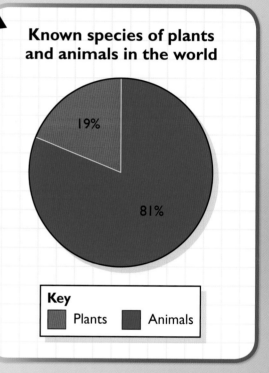

**Known species of plants and animals in the world**

19%

81%

**Key**
Plants   Animals

## Carroll diagrams

A Carroll diagram can be used to display and categorize information clearly and simply. It looks a bit like a table.

### Ecosystems and habitats on land or in water

|  | Land | Water |
|---|---|---|
| **Ecosystems** | Forest<br>Desert<br>Grassland<br>Mountain | Ocean<br>Lake<br>River<br>Canal |
| **Habitats** | Tree<br>Lawn<br>Sand dune<br>Flower pot | Stream<br>Pond<br>Puddle<br>Bird bath |

# Bar charts

Bar charts are a good way to compare amounts of different things. Bar charts have a vertical **y-axis** showing the scale and a horizontal **x-axis** showing the different types of information. They can show one or more different types of bars.

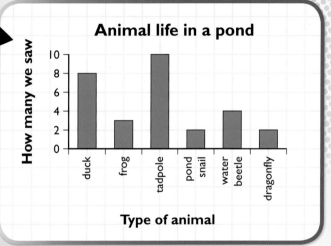

# Venn diagrams

A Venn diagram helps to organize information in order to compare two things. It has two circles, in two different colors, that overlap in the middle. In a Venn diagram, the separate parts of the circles show the differences between two things. The overlapping part of the circles show similarities.

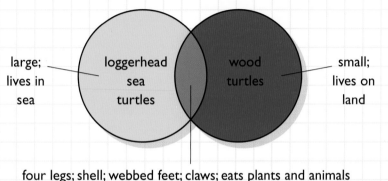

# Line graphs

Line graphs use lines to connect points on a graph. They can be used to show how something changes over time. Several lines on one line graph means that you can compare the overall pattern of several sets of data. Time, such as months, is usually shown on the x-axis.

# GLOSSARY

**adaptation** process by which plants and animals change over time so that they can survive in their habitat

**carnivore** animal that eats other animals

**conservation** protection of habitats, plants, and animals from damage

**consumer** animal that gets its energy by eating green plants or other consumers

**data** information, often in the form of numbers

**decomposer** organism that breaks down dead animals and plants into nutrients that go back into the earth

**deforestation** destroying forests by cutting them down

**ecosystem** community of organisms and the environment they live in, such as a wood or an ocean

**extinct** having died out forever as a species

**food chain** relationship between different organisms, showing who eats what. Food chains include producers and consumers.

**food web** series of food chains that are linked to each other

**fungus** (more than one are called fungi) type of plant that does not have green leaves, such as mold or mushrooms

**grassland** large area covered with grass

**herbivore** animal that eats plants

**industry** businesses and activities that produce goods for sale

**lichen** plant organism that grows, especially on rocks, walls, and trees

**mammal** animal that produces young as babies, not eggs. Mammals feed their young on milk from their own body.

**mate** partner that an animal needs to produce young

**native** plants or animals that grow naturally in a place, and that have not been brought there from somewhere else

**nutrient** substance needed by plants and animals to live and grow

**omnivore** animal that eats both plants and other animals

**organism** single living thing—either a plant or an animal

**polar region** area at the most northern and most southern points of Earth

**pollution** damage caused to the air, land, or water by harmful substances or garbage

**population** group of the same species of organism living in the same place at the same time

**predator** animal that hunts, kills, and eats other animals for food

**prey** animal that a predator kills for food

**producer** green plant that can make its own food from sunlight and water

**rain forest** thick forest in an area where a lot of rain falls. Many rain forests are found in the tropics.

**species** group of plants or animals that are similar to each other in important ways

**wetland** large area of land that is very wet and soft

**x-axis** horizontal line on a graph

**y-axis** vertical line on a graph

# FURTHER INFORMATION

## Books

Bellamy, Rufus. *Action for the Environment: Protecting Habitats*. Mankato, Minn.: Smart Apple Media, 2005.

Pipe, Jim. *Planet Earth: Earth's Ecosystems*. Milwaukee: Gareth Stevens, 2007.

Spilsbury, Louise. *The War in Your Backyard: Life in an Ecosystem*. Chicago: Raintree, 2006.

Wallace, Holly. *Life Processes: Food Chains and Webs*. Chicago: Heinemann Library, 2007.

## Websites

National Geographic Kids has information on creating and protecting habitats where you live.
www.nationalgeographic.com/ngkids/0304

The United Nations Environment Program, known as Pachamama, has information about the environment and what you can do to protect it.
www.unep.org/geo2000/pacha

The World Wildlife Fund has a section about various habitats for you to explore.
www.panda.org/news_facts/education/middle_school/habitats

# INDEX